February 1997

Welcome Rikky!

Uncle Joe
Aunt Nancy
Cousins
Charcoal
Twig
Kady

HOLLYWOOD
CATS

EDITED BY J.C. SUARÈS

CollinsPublishersSanFrancisco

A Division of HarperCollins*Publishers*

First published 1993 by Collins Publishers San Francisco

Copyright © 1993 J.C. Suarès

Captions copyright © 1993 Jane R. Martin

Additional copyright information page 80

Picture Research and Permissions: S.D. Evans

Library of Congress Cataloging-in-Publication Data

Hollywood cats/edited by J.C. Suarès

p. cm.

ISBN 0-00-255217-5

1. Cats in motion pictures--Pictorial works. 2. Motion picture actors and actresses--

Pictorial works. I. Suarès, Jean-Claude.

PN1995.9.A5H64 1993

791.43'66--dc20   11 93-18218 CIP

THE INCREDIBLE SHRINKING MAN. 1957
*Having shrunk to two inches tall, Grant Williams moved into
the dollhouse where he was hunted by the family cat, his worst
enemy aside from a six-inch Panamanian spider. Special
effects and split-screen editing weren't the only tricks used by
director Jack Arnold in this thriller. Arnold photographed the
furious cat hunting a little bird kept safely off-camera, and
then back-projected the cat through the window. A giant paw
was also used.*

The busiest cats in Hollywood history were Orangey and Morris. They were both short-haired orange tigers, well-fed, fluffy and photogenic. Orangey's career lasted from 1952 to 1963. Morris made his television debut in 1969 and died in 1978.

You might think from seeing their pictures that they came from the same litter but nothing was further from the truth. They looked like relatives but their off-stage personalities were poles apart.

Orangey was a cantankerous prima donna disliked even by his trainer. A movie executive called him "The World's Meanest Cat." During one shooting session, his trainer, Frank Inn, placed guard dogs at all the movie studio doors in order to dissuade the cat from running away.

However, Orangey was a real talent and according to Inn could "play any part" and won more awards than any other cat in show business before or since.

Orangey's big break came in 1952 when he played the title role in Paramount's *Rhubarb*, about a cat who inherits a fortune and buys the Brooklyn Dodgers. The movie, based on a 1950 novel of the same title by H. Allen Smith, starred Ray Milland, Jan Sterling and Gene Lockhart. The role landed Orangey the 1952 Patsy Award, which he won again ten years later for his role as "Cat" in Truman Capote's *Breakfast at Tiffany's* starring Audrey Hepburn and George Peppard. He also appeared in *Gigot* with Jackie Gleason and was a regular on the *Our Miss Brooks* television series starring Eve Arden as the sharp-tongued schoolteacher and Gale Gordon as the apoplectic principal.

Morris, the finnicky salesman of 9-Lives cat food, was as cool and charismatic as Orangey was mean spirited. He was almost certainly the most famous stray cat who ever lived. He was discovered in 1968 at the Humane

Society of Hinsdale, Illinois. When noted animal trainer Bob Martwick visited the shelter on a talent hunt for a mattress manufacturer, Morris was living in a cramped cage on the Humane Society's death row. If Martwick hadn't come along when he did, Morris might very well have been put to sleep to make room for more recent arrivals. But the star-to-be was almost impossible to distract; Martwick spotted his natural talent and paid five dollars for his release.

Later in the year, Morris beat out an enormous field of furry hopefuls to win a place in a planned advertising campaign for 9-Lives cat food. Morris was so exceptionally poised that the ad campaign was quickly rewritten to feature him as a star. The commercial's producers had never seen anything like him before. He was given his name (up until this point he had been known as Lucky) and star billing. Later, he was made an honorary director of Star-Kist Foods, Inc., 9-Lives' parent company, and was given the power to veto new cat-food flavors.

Morris was such an unprecedented phenomenon that he was given a special Patsy Award for "outstanding performance in a TV commercial" in 1973. He was chosen to co-star with Dyan Cannon and Burt Reynolds in the popular movie *Shamus.*

Like most celebrities, Morris found that his lifestyle followed his fortunes in the acting world. Once nothing more than a humble stray, he now found himself being invited to appear on countless television shows. He ate at fancy restaurants and hobnobbed with Hollywood stars. He even visited the White House and signed a bill making an ink impression with his paw. No cat has ever gone so far from such humble beginnings or been loved by so many.

J.C. Suarès

BELL, BOOK AND CANDLE. 1958
A feline-eyed Kim Novak holds Pyewacket the Siamese as she
brews up a witch's plot to win James Stewart's love. The cat
won a Patsy Award—the American Humane Association's
Picture Animal Top Star of the Year award—for his
performance.

THE BLACK CAT. 1934
*Bela Lugosi co-starred with
Boris Karloff for the first time
in this loose adaptation of
Edgar Allan Poe's story of a cat
returning from the dead to
haunt its master. The movie
wound up having more to do
with a story by director Edgar
Ulmer than with Poe's tale,
though a sleek black cat did
appear. The title was changed
to* The Vanishing Body *when
Universal released a second*
Black Cat *in 1941.*

THE BLUE BIRD. 1976
*This tuxedo-patterned Domestic American Longhair starred in
20th Century Fox's remake of this children's tale filmed in
Moscow. Elizabeth Taylor, Cicely Tyson, and Jane Fonda were
among the other stars in the lavish fantasy.*

JEAN HARLOW AND KITTENS. 1931
Above: *A non-platinum Harlow holds a trio of startled Persians.*

I MARRIED A WITCH. 1942
Left: *Veronica Lake starred in René Clair's comedy of a fetching witch who places a curse on the Puritan family that burns her, only to return two hundred years later and fall in love with its descendant. In the movie the enormous cat runs in the house and right into Lake's lap. It fell asleep during the photo session.*

PETER LORRE AND SIAMESE. 1944
While filming The Mask of Dimitrios *with Sydney Greenstreet*
for Warner Brothers, Peter Lorre poses with two Seal-point
Siamese kittens on his shoulders.

RHUBARB, 1951

H. Allen Smith's tale of a cat inheriting a baseball team was turned into a movie with many stars: Ray Milland, Jan Sterling, Gene Lockhart, and Leonard Nimoy. But the feline star, Orangey, stole the show and the awards—in his case, the 1952 Patsy. An intractable ginger tabby, he tried the patience of owner-trainer Frank Inn at almost every scene, harassing his stand-ins and running off the set with no warning.

MARLON BRANDO AT HOME. 1955
The brooding star of The Wild One *at home with his white cat,*
a Domestic American Shorthair.

JEAN PARKER. 1930s
One of the co-stars of George Cukor's Little Women *holds a tiny kitten.*

BREAKFAST AT TIFFANY'S. 1961

Above and left: *Defining cat irascibility for all movies to come, Orangey method-acted his way through the Audrey Hepburn-George Peppard romance in trademark style. As "Cat," Holly Golightly's "poor slob without a name," Orangey jumped onto the back of his hungover mistress to wake her up, and then leaped from the floor to Peppard's shoulders to a nearby shelf.*

EYE OF THE CAT. 1969
Previous pages: *Michael Sarrazin, Gayle Hunnicutt, and
Eleanor Parker starred in this suspenseful drama about an
aunt with a houseful of terrifying cats. Trainers use reward
methods to convince felines to act; punishment won't work.
One trick that's easy for cats to learn is lifting their paws.*

MONSIEUR VERDOUX. 1947
Right: *As a modern-day French Bluebeard, Charles Chaplin
also took pity on stray cats and sponsored a young ingénue,
played by Marilyn Nash. Here, a stray kitten dangles from
Nash's arms.*

ANTHONY PERKINS. 1959
The star of Psycho *plays with his cat.*

THE ADVENTURES OF MILO AND OTIS. 1989
Above: *The American release of this Japanese film about the misadventures of Milo, a tabby kitten, and Otis, a Pug puppy, was narrated by Dudley Moore. Eighteen animal trainers worked under animal supervisor Mikio Hata on the production.*

THE WRONG BOX. 1966
Right: *In this comedy about inheritance, Peter Sellers played the mad surgeon Dr. Pratt, his office overrun by kittens. As one cat sits in the surgical bowl, the doctor contemplates the phony death certificate he's just made out for Michael Caine.*

JUNE LOCKHART AND
THE FAMILY CAT. 1963
*During her stint as the mother
in the television series, Lassie,
the actress took a dip in her
Hollywood pool along with one
of the family cats. This one
learned to swim from
Lockhart's children.*

CAT'S EYE. 1985
*Stephen King's trilogy starred a silver tabby and
Drew Barrymore. The cat, named Lucky, Sebastian, and then
General, was trained by Karl Lewis Miller and
Teresa Ann Miller.*

NANCY WALKER. 1975
Rhoda's mother and the star of Bounty paper towel
commercials shares an elegant moment with her loving
Abyssinian.

THE SHADOW OF THE CAT. 1961
A black cat seeks revenge for her owner's murder.

ZIEGFELD GIRL. 1941
*The story of three actresses—played by Lana Turner, Hedy
Lamarr, and Judy Garland—featured giant Busby Berkeley
numbers with women emerging from oysters with pearls at
their feet and Persians in their laps.*

ALIEN. 1979
*Sigourney Weaver, in the first of the series, plays warrant
officer Ripley on the spaceship Nostromo. Readying her escape
from the indestructible creature that's taken over, she discovers
Jones the cat in his hideout, and hugs him with great relief.*

MR. AND MRS. ERNIE KOVACS. 1960s
The great comedian and his wife Edie Adams, who starred in
It's a Mad Mad Mad Mad World, *at home with their pet*
Persian.

URSULA ANDRESS. 1962
Above: *The co-star of the first James Bond movie,* Dr. No, *with Sean Connery, holds an Oriental Shorthair.*

JOAN COLLINS. 1957
Right: *A straw-hatted Joan Collins holds a kitten in her shirt during the filming of* Island in the Sun.

EYE OF THE CAT. 1969
*In another scene from the Universal thriller, Gayle Hunnicutt
is terrified by the cats as they surround her.*

MORRIS. 1970s

Above: *The giant orange tabby, who earned fame as the spokescat for 9-Lives cat food, was discovered in 1968 by noted animal trainer Bob Martwick at the Humane Society in Hinsdale, Illinois. That same year Morris beat out a huge field of contestants for the 9-Lives spot, and the ad campaign was rewritten to feature him as a star. He won a special Patsy award in 1973, and died wealthy in 1978.*

RHUBARB. 1951

Right: *The heir to the Brooklyn Dodgers is the center of attention in the courtroom. Paramount listed Rhubarb as being played by himself, but Orangey, the cat who played the title role, was a true actor, according to his trainer Frank Inn: "…best in the world, and can play any part."*

NOSFERATU THE VAMPYRE. 1979
The beautiful Isabelle Adjani as Lucy with her kitten. Klaus
Kinski played the Count.

GINA LOLLOBRIGIDA, 1950s
Philippe Halsman posed the Italian star with a Persian.

THE ADVENTURES OF MILO AND OTIS. 1989
Above: *In this Japanese film, Otis, a Pug puppy, sets out to rescue Milo, a tabby kitten who has been swept away by a rushing river.*

HARRY & TONTO. 1974
Right: *A bittersweet comedy about an old man, played by Art Carney, who travels across the country with his cat Tonto. In the story, the ginger tabby had his own suitcase and leash and purred when scolded.*

ANN-MARGRET. 1964
*Ann-Margret was presented with a Siamese kitten during the
filming of* Kitten with a Whip, *which had nothing to do with
cats but featured the actress as the leader of a gang that forces
John Forsythe's character to drive them to Mexico.*

MR. AND MRS. JAMES MASON AT HOME. 1940S
Above: *The star of* Fire Over England *and* The Seventh Veil
admires a litter of kittens with his wife.

BETTY GARRETT AND LARRY PARKS. 1948
Right: *Larry Parks starred in* The Jolson Story *before
blacklisting put an end to his Hollywood career.*

CAROLE LOMBARD. 1930S
*A silky portrait of the greatest of the screwball heroines on a
chaise longue with a black Persian.*

THAT DARN CAT. 1965
Hayley Mills poses with her co-star, an enormous Siamese named DC, that leads the FBI to the rescue. The actress also starred in The Parent Trap *movie series.*

NO SAD SONGS FOR ME. 1950
*In this saga of a family and its dying mother, played by
Margaret Sullavan, Natalie Wood sits with the family's black
shorthaired cat. Wood starred in* Rebel Without a Cause *five
years later.*

OLIVIA DE HAVILLAND. 1940S
Above: *The star of* The Adventures of Robin Hood *and* Gone
With the Wind *poses with her well-fed Siamese at home.*

AVA GARDNER. 1946
Right: *The star of* Whistle Stop *and* The Killers *by the pool
with her Siamese. These Oriental cats were highly popular in
Hollywood, prized for their exotic bearings and vocal,
animated personalities.*

BELL, BOOK AND CANDLE. 1958
*James Stewart looks with amazement at Kim Novak's feline
ally, Pyewacket, who is asleep in the witch's arms.*

CAT PEOPLE. 1942

*Jane Randolph comforts the kitten that's been mewing away in
a box all day. Presented by Kent Smith to his mysterious
girlfriend, Simone Simon, the kitten hissed with terror and had
to be taken away—the first hint that Simon had an uneasy
connection with the feline world. Brought to the office, the cat
does fine with thoroughly human Randolph.*

RHUBARB. 1951
*At fourteen pounds, Orangey
the cat had enough presence to
look imposing on a baseball
diamond, but the camera angle
helped. The leash was there in
case the star decided to bolt.*

THE BLACK CAT. 1941
Universal's second version of the Edgar Allen Poe story, a comedy-chiller, also featured Bela Lugosi. He played the caretaker for a woman who kept a crematorium for her beloved cats. Anne Gwynne played an innocent victim haunted at midnight by the feline villain.

LAUREN BACALL. 1940s
The new Warner Brothers star poses with a black cat.

ON HER MAJESTY'S SECRET SERVICE. 1969
Telly Savalas played Ernst Stavros Blofeld, the head of
SPECTRE, *in the only James Bond movie to star George Lazenby.*

THE GODFATHER. 1972
*Marlon Brando won an unaccepted Oscar for his role as
Don Corleone.*

PEPPER THE CAT, 1920S

The gray cat climbed up through a broken floorboard and right into Mack Sennett's Hollywood studio, where she was immediately installed in the scene being shot. She performed beautifully. Sennett christened her Pepper and made her the feline star of many silents. Her curiosity made her a fast learner. She picked up checkers instantly to play with comedian Ben Turpin, and formed a lasting partnership with Teddy, the Sennett studio's Great Dane. In mourning for the departed dog, she ended her career just as she'd started it— by refusing to stay on the set.

PHOTOGRAPHIC ACKNOWLEDGMENTS

3: Courtesy The Kobal Collection
9: Photofest
10-11: Photofest
13: Photofest
14: Courtesy The Kobal Collection
15: Photofest
16: Everett Collection
17: Photofest
19: Photofest
21: Archive Photos
22: Courtesy The Kobal Collection
23: Courtesy The Kobal Collection
24-25: Everett Collection
27: Everett Collection
29: Photo by © Sid Avery/Courtesy Motion Picture & Television Photo Archive
30: Photofest
31: Photofest
32-33: Everett Collection
34: Courtesy The Kobal Collection
35: Archive Photos
37: Everett Collection
39: Courtesy The Kobal Collection
40: Courtesy The Kobal Collection
41: Photofest
43: Archive Photos
44: Archive Photos

45: Archive Photos
47: Courtesy The Kobal Collection
48: Courtesy Star-Kist Foods, Inc.
49: Culver Pictures
51: Everett Collection
53: Photofest
55: Photo by Philippe Halsman © Yvonne Halsman
56: Courtesy The Kobal Collection
57: Culver Pictures
59: Archive Photos
60: Archive Photos
61: Archive Photos
63: Courtesy The Kobal Collection
64: Photofest
65: Photofest
66: Archive Photos
67: Archive Photos
68: Courtesy The Kobal Collection
69: Courtesy The Kobal Collection
70-71: Courtesy The Kobal Collection
73: Courtesy The Kobal Collection
75: Courtesy Motion Picture & Television Photo Archive
76: Everett Collection
77: Courtesy The Kobal Collection
78: Everett Collection
Back Cover: Archive Photos